Many people are disc
don't know and grow
passionate and pract ... will help to encourage every believer in your journey. If you don't know The Word you will not grow! Digest The Word everyday and it will change your life as you grow and are encouraged!

Reverend Lee E. Cooper, Jr.
Senior Pastor, Prospect Church

Here's a devotional pick-me-up for every woman's soul. Feeling discouraged? Overjoyed? Stressed? Alice offers radical truth of mind for radical change of heart.

Pam Kanaly
Author/Speaker, National Mother of Achievement,
Co-founder of Arise Ministries -America's leading
advocate for single mothers - ariseministries.net

I believe that the Word of God is timeless and relevant even today. Radically Living the Word Devotional is an easy read. It provides engaging examples that help us relate our life experiences to God's Word.

Cuonzo Martin
Head Coach of the University of California Golden
Bears Men's Basketball Team

5 stars

We must all fall to our knees and give it over to God. Too often we take over the reins of our lives and try to work things out the way we want. Richardson has done a masterful job of integrating the practicality of God's Word into the daily meditations. She uses her anointed spirit and has honestly written a translation of the scriptures through her daily conversations with God. She does not shrink from the real issues we often struggle with rather she speaks to them head on. Each devotional has a summary and Let's Agree section that provide invaluable wisdom along with her personal experiences. This devotional speaks encouragement to the soul and rededication for your heart.

The scriptures analyzed in this work offer answers to life's problems. This book shows people how the Bible helps them live to be the spirit filled productive lives God called them to be. I highly recommend this book to everyone with a desire to grow closer to God.

Monique "Deltareviewer" Bruner

This wonderful Book of Meditations covers a wide range of relevant Biblical themes, will resonate, connect and help most 21st Century Christians who are hungering and thirsting for righteousness. The themes include unavoidable life issues like anger, fear, forgiveness, love, patience, and a host of other life issues with which many Christians struggle. When we meditate on these kinds of issues they help us to talk God's kind of talk, walk His kind of walk and teach His ways in our world. The Word in Ephesians 4:1 says: "Live in a way that is worthy of the people God has chosen to be His own." (Contemporary English Version) So, read, study, and meditate on the messages of this book; they will inspire you to go where the Spirit leads and be blessed!

Mark Green Sr.
Retired Senior Pastor of the African Methodist Episcopal Church; Past President of the New Bedford, Massachusetts Branch of the NAACP.

Radically Living the Word is a powerful, scripture based devotional with encouraging words for the heart. This book is great for new Christians, as well as those who want to re-dedicate themselves to GOD. If you have found yourself neglecting your spiritual health Minister Alice Richardson provides a firm foundation to help you jump-start your spiritual life. She provides a wonderful compilation of scriptures, teaching, and real life lessons that will fortify your life. Then she summarizes each lesson with inspiring prayers of agreement.

Rich in ideas and examples, this treatise re-enforces how important prayer and studying the Word are to our everyday life. Alice's book gave me "cheat sheets" of steps I could take to move forward in my relationship with God.

Rashun Jones
Registered Nurse, Author, Speaker

Radically Living the Word

Daily Encouragement Devotional Series
Volume 1

Radically Living the Word

Daily Encouragement Devotional Series
Volume 1

Encouragement is a game changer. Let God's Word be the difference maker in your life today!

Alice T. Richardson

ISBN-13: 978-0-9964476-0-7

Library of Congress Control Number: 2015909562

Please visit the website at
www.alicerichardson.org
Online ordering is available.

Published by Alice Richardson
P.O. Box 6952
Edmond, OK 73083

DEDICATION

With great joy, I dedicate this volume to my mother,
Patricia Michelle Clark.
Memories of your love continue to inspire the best in me.

CONTENTS

Contents

Contents

ACKNOWLEDGMENTS

I give honor to my God for His infinite goodness and mercy. Father, you have been so very patient with me as I have written for many years without taking the publishing step. Thank you, Lord, for this day!

To my wonderful husband, Micheal, who has taken this journey with me; your daily encouragement is priceless. You truly are my special gift from the Savior.

Alexandria and Joshua, my wonderful children, who continue to believe in what's best in me; know that I believe in you too. You are truly amazing people!

To my Aunts: Katherine, Lena, Rosetta, and Syretha and to my "second chance" Mom, Mary Bratcher, thank you for your continual love and support.

For being a worthy friend, a sister, a faithful traveling companion and someone who encouraged me to write, Marsha Beasley, thank you.

Rashun Jones, I appreciate your consistent willingness, even eagerness, to share your writing experience with me. You are a remarkable author!

To my Editor, for your constant enthusiasm and expert direction, thank you.

And to my wonderful spiritual family at Prospect Church who share life-giving encouragement...Thank You!

Make every effort to apply God's promises to your life, it will produce a life of moral excellence. A life of moral excellence leads to knowing God better.
2 Peter 1:5

Introduction

I learned early in life that everyday does not bring sunshine. There are days when I felt disappointment, days when I experienced grief, and days when I was angry. As the years passed, I began to understand that it is not what happens to me that shapes my future; it is the way that I process and deal with what happens. The reality is that life is a series of tests. Test that help develop us into the strong, devil-defeating men and women that God created us to be. So do not be weary of the daily challenges, instead see them as stepping stones to your next level of glory!

My friend, whether you are a new Christian or have served God most of your life, this small book will give you the spiritual lift that you need to see God in every situation. Whether the day brings sunshine (kids making you proud, promotion on your job, fulfilling relationships) or rain (sickness, financial difficulty, divorce) you can stand strong on the Word of God.

Join me in the pages of this motivating work and find hope through authoritative Scriptures, transformative words of encouragement, and inspiring prayers of agreement. It will inspire and help you to make LIVING the Bible a lifestyle! It's practical, brief, and written in everyday language.

To make your experience more meaningful, I suggest that you start by paying attention to every title. Do not just breeze by them; intentionally read them. Next spend a moment meditating on the Scripture. Read it slowly twice before moving on. Then, carefully read the day's message. Finally, pray the prayer sincerely as though your Heavenly Father was sitting in front of you, your hands gently held in His while He listens intently to every word of your prayer. In reality, He is! He hears every word that you say and feels what you feel. He cares about you and promises to make all the difficult situations you go through work together for your good! Therefore, as you move through the pages of this devotional, confidently and intentionally confess your victory over every situation. My prayer is for your relationship with your Creator to grow and your problems to shrink!

Radically Living the Word

Daily Encouragement Devotional Series
Volume 1

I weep with sorrow;
encourage me by your word.
Psalm 119:28

Grace Received And Grace Given

"So now there is no condemnation for those who belong to Christ Jesus." (Romans 8:1)

I once heard that each day is new with no mistakes in it! Step into today with the new grace that God has reserved just for you. Romans 8:1 says we no longer live condemned, sad, and hopeless lives. If you believe in your heart and confess with your mouth that God has raised Jesus from the dead, you are now a divine foreign exchange student, living on earth, but your citizenship is heaven. Jesus destroyed sin's control over our lives! Today give yourself the same grace that God gives you. While you are at it, share that grace with the people in your life who may not "deserve" it, but desperately need it. Jesus was crucified for you and me. Today let's crucify our desire to use our mouths to hurt others. We can do it with His help!

Let's agree: Dear Heavenly Father, thank You for the awesome power that accompanies earnest prayer. Help me to walk in Your Holy Spirit today, replacing cutting words with healing words of reconciliation and encouragement. Amen!

Weakness Turned To Strength

"Each time He said, 'My grace is all you need. My power works best in weakness.' So now I am glad to boast about my weakness, so that the power of Christ can work through me. That's why I take pleasure in my weakness, and in the insults, hardships, persecutions, and troubles that I suffer for Christ. For when I am weak, then I am strong." (2 Corinthians 12:9- 10)

Today you may have numerous challenges looming before you, but remind your soul that THIS too shall pass. No matter how it looks, God promises strength for weakness. When you sense that you are getting overwhelmed today, take three deep slow breathes (in through the nose, out through the mouth). You have an awesome God that is on your side! Testify to yourself by remembering how He has come through in the past. He will do it again! In Second Corinthians 12:9-10 Paul finds pleasure even in his hardships because God's power works best in human weakness. Your challenges are the necessary environment for God's miraculous power!

Let's agree: Father, today I declare that I am healed in my body and my mind. I am not discouraged by the challenges in my life; instead I am ENCOUAGED because I understand that life's challenges set the atmosphere for miracles! Amen!

Weekend Warfare

"Keep watch and pray, so that you will not give in to temptation. For the spirit is willing, but the body is weak!" (Matthew 26:41)

"Stay alert! Watch out for your great enemy, the devil. He prowls around like a roaring lion, looking for someone to devour." (1 Peter 5:8)

The weekend! For most, it means time off work. It's an opportunity to do your own thing, make your own schedule, get your swag on, or get your groove back. On the weekend we often let our guard down. We unwind. Resting is a necessary part of our lives, so go ahead and relax! Just don't forget that the battle for your peace, health, marriage, purity, sanity...your life, rages on. Satan never takes a day off! So, although we rest physically, we remain spiritually alert, for the adversary roams about like a lion seeking those he can devour. (Matthew 26:41; 1 Peter 5:8) Therefore, don't forget to schedule a date with God this weekend. Spend time with Him in His Word, in worship, and in prayer. Nothing says "I love you" like time.

Let's agree: Dearest Father, there are days I feel like nothing could go wrong, other days it seems nothing will go right. I thank You for every up *and* down because they teach me a little more about being both grateful and humble. Thank you Father that the downs are never lower than I could bear and the ups never so high that I forget to be grateful. Lord, I love and trust You. Help me to be mindful to engage in weekend warfare. Amen!

Misplaced Promises

"Study this Book of Instruction continually. Meditate on it day and night so you will be sure to obey everything written in it. Only then will you prosper and succeed in all you do." (Joshua 1:8)

Have you ever found money in a suit or coat pocket? Or perhaps it was some other valued item that you inadvertently left somewhere? You do not miss it because you forget you had it. It is only after you find it again that you remember it was misplaced. God has given us powerful, precious promises. However, in the activity of life we can lose track of them, tucking them away. We do not intentionally do this, it just happens. Life is so busy that we fail to even notice that the real power of life is gone. We are left muddling along in our own power, instead of confidently standing on the promises of God. This is not a profound revelation, but believers often don't remember the promises until trouble shows up, then we pull them out like a gunfighter in the Wild West. God desires us to meditate on His promises daily. Memorize them. Get them in our heart. He wants us to let them interrupt the negative thoughts that regularly assault our minds. This week determine to recall and declare God's divine promises over your life and the members of your family! Here's one to get you started!

Commit your plans to the Lord and He will bring them to good success. (Proverbs 16:3)

Let's agree: Father, You remember Your covenant forever, the promises You made You remember for a thousand generations! Give me the desire and courage to recall and declare Your promises with conviction. Father, right now I speak LIFE over my life and over all that concerns me! In Jesus' Name, AMEN!

A Big Mouth Can Lead to Big Trouble

"Don't use foul or abusive language. Let everything you say be good and helpful, so that your words will be an encouragement to those who hear them." (Ephesians 4:29)

How carefully do you monitor your words? Do you monitor them at all or do you just say whatever comes into your mind? Our words are powerful! Using your mouth is like driving your car. It's great if you use it responsibly, but it also holds the potential for some major wrecks if handled carelessly. God tells us not to let any unwholesome talk come out of our mouths, but only what is helpful for building others up according to their needs, that it may benefit those who listen. Are people around you benefiting from listening to what you say? Are your children learning to use words to help or hurt, respect or disrespect? Your words say more about who YOU are, than the person you may bad mouth. So, if gossip is a challenge, work on limiting your words this week. If foul language is a problem, take one of those words out of your vocabulary... permanently. Use your words this week to say something good about yourself, by encouraging someone else. Start today!

Let's agree: Father, your purpose for words is to encourage and give life. Help me to speak life or bridle my tongue. In Jesus' Name, AMEN!

God Is Looking For You

"The eyes of the Lord search the whole earth in order to strengthen those whose hearts are fully committed to him." (2 Chronicles 16:9a)

Need a blessing? Then God is looking for you! He is moving to and fro in the earth looking for someone He can heal, someone He can encourage, someone He can deliver! No matter where you are in life; no matter what season you are in, you are never out of His reach or out of His sight. Only question is, are you blocking the blessings God is trying to give you? You are likely thinking, of course not! But do you understand what blocks blessings? No, it's not your mean boss or the Internal Revenue Service (IRS). It's sin. Sin separates us from God. (Isaiah 59:2) It serves as a big gulf between us. Repentance, however, bridges the gap. It is, therefore, important for believers to regularly go before God and ask forgiveness for sins committed. This is necessary because salvation does not prevent us from making sinful mistakes, it provides us a way to be cleansed once we repent of them. Is there unrepentant sin active in your life? Are there places you enjoy going and things you enjoy doing that give you temporary happiness, but block you from receiving authentic blessings from our heavenly Father? You may have found your current dating partner in a place you shouldn't have been or attracted them by doing something you shouldn't have done, so are they *really* God's choice for you? You may have gotten the money to pay the rent, but is God pleased with your methods? We all sin and fall short of God's glory, but sin should not be allowed to linger or to become an unrepentant lifestyle. Do you need a blessing? Take a moment and examine your life for willful and unrepentant sin. Cross over the bridge of repentance and discover the blessings on the other side of your obedience!

Let's agree: Father, please forgive me for the times I have carefully thought out my sinful behaviors and activities. Today, I repent of every blessing blocker in my life: unforgiveness, lying, hate, sexual sin, and every other thing that separates me from You. I love you Lord and choose to please You. Thank You in advance for the amazing blessings You are sending my way. In Jesus' Name, AMEN!

Stop Worry In Its Tracks

"Don't worry about anything; instead, pray about everything. Tell God what you need, and thank Him for all He has done. Then you will experience God's peace, which exceeds anything we can understand. His peace will guard your hearts and minds as you live in Christ Jesus." (Ephesians 4:6, 7)

Stop worrying! God's got your back. Easier said than done, right? But let God's powerful Word ring through the corridors of your heart and mind today. "Don't worry!" Worry can quickly overtake us and steal our joy. But what causes worry? Fear. What causes us to be afraid? Most of the time, it involves not seeing the end of a situation from the beginning; the unknowns of life. Our heavenly Father is asking us to trust Him with the unforeseeable future, because He sees the beginning and the end. Think about it, when you head off to work, you don't usually worry about your arrival; mainly because you know the address of your destination, you know the route, and you've likely made the trip before, possibly many times. But when we embark upon the journey through a trial, all we know is the beginning. The unknown details can cause us to stress out and exchange our faith for fear. How should we deal with the unknowns? God says by talking to Him. He knows all things and He is willing to lovingly guide us through every trial. Take some time to pray and He promises to give you peace that no one can understand.

Let's agree: Father, I know that trials do not come to destroy me, but to make me strong. Help me to exchange my fear for faith, not my faith for fear. In Jesus' Name, AMEN!

A Firm Foundation For A Strong Self-Esteem

"You made all the delicate, inner parts of my body and knit me together in my mother's womb. Thank You for making me so wonderfully complex! Your workmanship is marvelous—how well I know it. How precious are Your thoughts about me, O God. They cannot be numbered!" (Psalm 139:13-14, 17)

Is your self-esteem a little battered? How do you really feel about yourself today? Much of the time we determine how we feel about ourselves by how other people treat us. Other times our self-esteem is driven by what we have going on in our lives. If everything is going well at work, with the kids, with school, with our significant other, then we often feel pretty good about ourselves. But connecting something as vital as self-esteem to something as volatile as emotions and performance is unwise. Even our own emotions can betray us and make us get down on ourselves. Stop believing the lies that you hear internally (in your own mind) and externally (from others). Our God has the only opinion that matters and He conveys in His Word how very important you are to Him. He saw you before you were born and ordained all the days of your life before one of them came to be. His thoughts about you are precious; thoughts too numerous to count! HE loves you, shouldn't YOU love you? Begin today affirming the wonderful work you are! Check yourself out in the mirror and thank God for who you see. Walk away knowing your outer beauty is only a small measure of the beauty Almighty God sees in you!

Let's agree: Father, thank You for choosing me to be Your child. Your love for me is unquestionable and unquenchable! It was for me that Jesus came and died. Nothing else is necessary to prove my significance. Thank you Lord, AMEN!

Best Date Ever

"The Word of the Lord holds true, and we can trust anything He does." (Psalm 33:4)

"Don't love money; be satisfied with what you have. For God has said, 'I will never fail you. I will never abandon you." (Hebrews 13:5)

Need a date? Thank God for Jesus! He is the best date ever! With Him, there is no drama. He's always faithful. (Psalm 33:4) He won't ever leave you nor forsake you. (Hebrews 13:5) He always leads you in the right direction, and never influences you to do wrong. There is never a need to compromise your standards for Him, and when the date is over there is no need for repentance. Your self-esteem is not damaged; as a matter of fact, it is improved! You don't need to worry about dressing up, just wear the robe of righteousness. Makeup is not an issue either; His attention is on your inner beauty. Finally, another amazing aspect of these dates with Jesus is that you can be married to someone else! Fact is, your relationship with the One in your heart can actually improve the relationship with the one in your bed. So, set a regular time and be on time for the best date ever!

Let's agree: Father, thank You for the blessing of prayer and for the power that accompanies time spent with You. My desire in life is to bear the fruit of love, joy, peace, kindness, patience, gentleness, goodness, faithfulness, and self-control. Therefore, Jesus, help me to abide in

Your presence so my life will be fruitful. Thank you Lord, AMEN!

Unavoidable Difficulty

"Who shall separate us from the love of Christ? Shall trouble or hardship or persecution or famine or nakedness or danger or sword? No, in all these things we are more than conquerors through Him who loved us." (Romans 8:35, 37)

Often when we consider the parable of the Good Samaritan (Luke 10:25-37) the perspective of the wounded and robbed traveler is overlooked. The traveling man had done nothing to contribute to his dreadful situation. He was just traveling from Jerusalem to Jericho. Bible scholars say the road he chose was known for its difficulty and danger, but it was obviously a road that he needed to take to get to his destination. He could have decided to avoid the journey due to the potential hardships. There were plenty other directions he could have taken, but he realized other directions would have led him to other places. So he resolved to go to Jericho even though it meant facing difficulty. On the way he did encounter hardship. He was injured and left to die by thieves (unbelievers). He was even deserted and rejected by a priest and a Levite (professed believers). Has rejection and pain been a part of your story? Today as you make your way to and from work, to the grocery store, or perhaps to pick up the kids at the nursery or school, you will try to find the "best" route to your destination. You will attempt to avoid the difficult roads that have potholes, frequent traffic accidents, and detours. Steering clear of these rough routes is a smart decision, but sometimes adversity is unavoidable, it's just a part of this piece of the journey. But like our traveler in Luke 10, you are not alone on your journey. Our heavenly Father is with you and He has people on assignment along the way who are poised to encourage and help you. They will anoint your wounds and help you get to a place of healing.

Let's agree: Almighty God, sometimes I feel lonely and left out. I have dealt with betrayal, deception, and loss. My heart is broken. Lord, anoint me, heal me, bind up my wounds and deliver me to a place of mental, physical, and spiritual restoration. In Jesus' Name, AMEN!

Don't Be Afraid, Be Strong

"This is My command—be strong and courageous! Do not be afraid or discouraged. For the Lord your God is with you wherever you go!" (Joshua 1:9)

Brothers, this one's especially for you. I can only imagine the challenges you face day to day. I am not a man, don't want to be a man, but I had a loving father, I have a loving husband, and I raised a responsible son. Watching them was like having a privileged view of the metamorphosis process of the caterpillar from the inside. I watched my dad struggle to stay sober, my husband struggle to adjust to me (no easy job), and my son struggle to "fit in" while maintaining an authentic relationship with God. These were a few of the struggles I recognized. I am sure there were others. In my counseling there is another recurring challenge I recognize in men. It is the challenge to lead their families, to be the head of their homes. They want to, they just don't know how. I share with each of them the fact that as a Christian, he must KNOW that since he is male, God has given him the ability to lead his own family. But...I also share that it will not be easy. In the beginning it was only Adam and Eve and looked what happened! So hang in there! Be encouraged! God has not given you (or will not give you) a family only to cut out on you leaving you to fend for yourself. His grace will cover you and His Holy Spirit will teach you. It is your job to seek the will of God for your family by learning and trusting His Word. It is also your job to keep your family covered in prayer. Additionally, a significant part of your job is to model godly attitudes and behaviors. Ultimately, brothers, if you want to be a powerful man you must be a self-disciplined man, an educated man, and a godly man. To be a boy in a man's body, simply do nothing. I encourage you, beloved, to build your home on the Rock and it will not be destroyed! (Matthew 7:24-27) Have faith brothers, and chances are your family will have faith too. There's a cost to manhood. That cost is DISCIPLINE. Are you willing to pay the price? (Joshua 1:6-9)

Let's agree: Thank you Father for godly men all over the world. Watch over them and build them up in Your Word. Father, I pray for my brothers who are praying with me right now. Give them the encouragement that they need to be who You created them to be; give them the strength required to discipline themselves to draw nigh to You; give them the joy of seeing each member of their families saved by Your awesome grace and living a healthy and prosperous life. In Jesus' Powerful Name, AMEN!

Check Your Diet Then Check Your Attitude

"How can a young person stay pure? By obeying Your Word. I have tried hard to find You—don't let me wander from Your commands. I have hidden Your Word in my heart, that I might not sin against You." (Psalm 119:9-11)

Do you enjoy eating? I do! There are so many delicious choices of appetizers, entrées, desserts, and snacks. Most of us consume foods based upon our taste, but it is important to know that we will eventually become what we eat. If we have a steady diet of junk food, our bodies will become weak and our minds sluggish. However, when we intentionally eat foods and choose drinks that promote health, we look and feel much better. But diet alone does not keep us healthy, there needs to be a commitment to exercise. Exercise refreshes the mind by supplying it with more oxygen. It improves our mood, blood circulation, alertness, memory, and core strength. Setting time aside to go to the gym or walk around your neighborhood can be the difference in aging gracefully or gracelessly. Is it easy? No! If we are not determined to exercise and eat right, it won't happen. There are too many distractions, other easier activities that we prefer over dieting and exercising. If we are not careful, excuses become our mantra. We can begin to talk ourselves out of being healthy, out of having the body we want. But health is not just a physical challenge; it is also a spiritual one. In the same way that our physical condition weakens for lack of proper nutrition and exercise, our spiritual condition weakens when we do not have proper spiritual nutrition and exercise (bible study, prayer, worship, listening to encouraging music, healthy fellowship, etc). Too many missed opportunities to be properly, spiritually fed, will make us lose spiritual definition and stamina. We can begin to believe previously rejected behaviors are now acceptable. People will get on our nerves quicker, we get angry faster, stay mad longer, and we can even refuse to forgive. When we fail to put our God's Word in our heart, we fail to position ourselves for daily victories. How's your diet? Truth is we all can do better. Make a decision to get physically and spiritually fit, starting today. Don't put it off. Difficult decisions don't become easier when delayed; you just miss out on the benefits that an earlier decision would have given. You can do it!

Let's agree: Father, help me to truly digest the fact that my physical condition can be no better than the investment I make in it; and my spirit will only be as strong as my commitment to spend time talking to You (prayer) and listening to You (studying Your Word). Help me to overcome the obstacles that hinder my progress. Undergird me in my weakness, hold my hand through the process, and multiply the benefits of my efforts. Thank You Lord, AMEN!

Think Right, Do Right

"And now, dear brothers and sisters, one final thing. Fix your thoughts on what is true, and honorable, and right, and pure, and lovely, and admirable. Think about things that are excellent and worthy of praise. Keep putting into practice all you learned and received from me—everything you heard from me and saw me doing. Then the God of peace will be with you." (Philippians 4:8-9)

Mistakes in behavior only follow mistakes in thinking. Sinful thoughts produce sinful behavior. Godly thoughts produce godly behavior. Thus, loving thoughts produce loving behavior; selfish thoughts, selfish behavior; mean thoughts, mean behavior; kind thoughts, kind behavior. You get the picture. If we think right, we will act right. When our thinking is beneath that of a Christian, our behavior will also be beneath that of a Christian. How do we get our minds right? Prayer and practice. "Fix your mind on what is true, good, and right. Think about things that are pure and lovely, and dwell on the fine, good things in others. Focus on everything you can praise our God for and celebrate. Keep putting into practice all that you have learned in His Word and it will bring you peace."

Let's agree: Father, I want to have the mind of Christ. Help me to fix my mind on what is true, good and right. As I put Your Word into practice daily, transform me by the renewing of my mind. Let my light shine that others will see my life and glorify You! In Jesus' Name, AMEN!

The Iron Chef Of Life

"And we know that all things work together for good to those who love God, to those who are the called according to His purpose." (Romans 8:28)

Rejoice and again I say rejoice! Today is another exciting day to be alive! It does not matter how many ups and downs you had this week or last week, what matters is by our God's amazing grace you made it through! Take the lessons you have learned and live wiser in the days to come. Don't look back and regret, don't reopen wounds, and don't curse the experience. Just take the good from it and move on. Be confident that our heavenly Father will use even THAT (the bad stuff) as one of the ingredients to produce an awesome future for you! (Jeremiah 29:11) He's the Iron Chef of life. He uses EVERYTHING, the desirable and undesirable ingredients of life, to create a good situation for you. How? I don't know. I just know He has done it again and again in the past, and He will do it again in the future. Why am I so sure about it? Because He never changes. His love, faithfulness, and power are the same love, faithfulness and power that opened the Red Sea to get His children out of a tough place. It is the same love that compelled our Savior to hang on Calvary's tree and the same power that raised Him from the dead. You can count on our heavenly Father. So, stop stressing. Be assured that while you are resting in Him, God is working to flip the script in your favor!

Let's agree: Father, You are awesome! There is none other like You. You are the Alpha and Omega, the beginning and the end. You are my fortress and strength, my Strong Deliverer. I rest in You, casting all of my cares upon You. Thank You for the trials of this week. Help me to learn the lessons and be better in the process. In Jesus' Name, AMEN!

Anger

"It is better to be slow-tempered than famous; it is better to have self-control than to control an army." (Proverbs 16:32 NLT)

Here is my translation of this Scripture: "Coming out of the bag" is not cute. Getting revenge never equals getting even. Being disrespected is a matter of perspective. Everyone's opinion of you shouldn't matter; it's not worth fighting over. Don't pay the cost attached to worthless things. Sometimes disrespect down here gains respect up there...what's most important? It's your choice; deciding your response now is much easier than waiting to decide once you are in a tough situation.

Let's agree: Dear Father, thank You for Your words of wisdom that guide me around the minefields of life. Help me to remember this Word, hiding it in my heart, so I can have strength in the battle. I don't want to pay the price for responding to worthless opinions, so help me to focus on the only opinion that matters...Yours. I am wonderfully made by You Father; Your love and acceptance are all I need. Amen!

Changelings

"As iron sharpens iron, so a friend sharpens a friend." (Proverbs 27:17)

Changelings. Do you know any? Are you one? You know, people who are one way in the morning and one way in the afternoon. On Saturday they are your friend, but on Tuesday they have issues with you. You can change for them, but they are so temperamental, so "iffy", that by the time you change to pacify them, they have changed again. How do you deal with that? You don't. There are literally billions of people in the world, hundreds of millions in America alone; do you really need a toxic person in your life? I don't. This is not a green light to behave beneath the expectation of our heavenly Father; we still represent Him. What it should do is release you from chasing unhealthy friendships. Assess the benefits. Are you better because of the relationship, or do find yourself depressed after contact with them? If you are better, check out the mirror and make sure the problem in the friendship isn't you. If you answered depressed, then consider reassigning that person to the associate files in your life. This means you are still kind and encouraging, and you treat them with love when you see them. You don't treat them with disdain or rush out of stores to avoid talking to them. Periodic assessment and reassignment of the people in our lives is simply a good relational principle. It keeps us from investing quality "friendship" time with people who are proven "associates." Good emotional health leads to better physical health and peace of mind. "Guard your heart above all else, for it determines the course of your life." (Proverbs 4:23)

Moving forward: Seek relationships that strengthen your moral, educational, professional and spiritual philosophies. God calls these "iron sharpening iron" relationships.

Let's agree: Father, You said that a friend loves at all times. Master, You are my best friend. You stick closer than a brother. You have been there in the good times and the tough times. When I make mistakes You don't mistreat me, You give me grace. When I am down, You lift me up! Lord, give me the courage to reassign the people in my life who are not good for my emotional health. Connect me with true friends who will help me be a better me. In Jesus' Name, AMEN!

Why Bother?

"While Jesus was still speaking, some people came from the house of Jairus, the synagogue leader. 'Your daughter is dead,' they said. 'Why bother the teacher anymore?' Overhearing what they said, Jesus told him, "Don't be afraid; just believe." (Mark 5:35, 36 NIV)

One of my favorite faith Scriptures is Mark 5:35, 36. Where the NIV says "just believe" the Amplified Bible says "only keep on believing." I like that! People are so quick to get into your business and even quicker to tell you what you need to do in your situation. In this text, a man's daughter was terribly sick and he was seeking the help of Jesus. His friends and family showed up to tell him that, from their perspective, his hopes were dead. They said just accept it and stop asking Jesus to help you. They didn't mean any harm; they just didn't understand the conviction of Jairus' faith or the power of Jesus. Jesus told Jarius to ignore their report and keep on believing. He tells us to do the same thing today. Don't believe everything everybody tells you, no matter how credible. Truth is, much of what we hear needs to be ignored. But don't get it twisted, walking in faith doesn't mean living with a bag on your head. It doesn't mean refusing to take medications the doctor prescribes. Our heavenly Father uses medical professionals every day. Take your medicine until your doctor says you don't need it any more. In this way the doctor himself testifies to the goodness of our God when he no longer sees a need for medication. Whatever the facts of your situation, deal with them, but in the process, don't stop believing our God for a miracle! *Deal with reality, but operate in faith.*

Let's agree: Father, thank You for the powerful examples of faith in Your Word. Give me the courage to ignore the naysayers and trust You in seemingly impossible situations. Help me to abide in Your presence and keep believing Your promises! In Jesus' Name, Amen!

Speak Life

"The tongue has the power of life and death." (Proverbs 18:21a)

Stated another way, our words have power to give life or to kill, it's our choice. Complaining kills...hopes and dreams, self-esteem, marriages, and anything else it consistently touches. Encouragement does the opposite. It can breathe life into dead hopes and dreams, restore self-image, and heal marriages. This is particularly true when the Words are God's. Here are some powerful affirmations that you can make that will change your life! Just believe!

"I am more than a conqueror today!" (Romans 8:37)

"Everything that is going on in my life today will work together to bless my life." (Romans 8:28)

"I am not discouraged, instead I am encouraged! My hope is my all powerful God. He will not fail me." (Romans 8:31-32)

"Heavenly Father, Your promises are manifesting in my spouse and children's lives today!" (Psalm 27:13)

"My heart rejoices in You today Father!" "I am healthy in soul, spirit, and body!" (Psalm 13: 4-6)

Let's agree: Father, I speak life over me and my family today. You said Your Word would not return unto You void. So, I get in agreement with Your Living Word right now, connecting my mustard seed faith with Your awesome promises. Help me to stop wasting my words with needless complaints; instead help me to declare

LIFE over my life every day! In Jesus' Magnificent Name, Amen!

For It Is Written

"Hide Your Word in my heart Lord, that I'll not sin against You." (Psalm 119:11)

Is this your prayer? I hope it is. It is my prayer; because the presence of God's Word in my heart leaves less room for sin. The heart is like a container. It holds whatever we put into it. We can hide both good things and bad things in it. The bad is sinful attitudes like lust, worry, and unforgiveness. The good is His Word that gives us peace, confidence, and a loving attitude. Sin weakens us. It steals our power, our joy, and our witness. The Word of God strengthens us and helps us in the battles of life. Do you need help? I do! God calls His Word the Sword of the Spirit. (Romans 8:17) It is our weapon against our adversary, the devil. Fill your heart with the Word and when the enemy attacks, pull out your mighty Sword and defeat him! "It is written..." (Luke 4:4, 8, 12)

Simply put:
No Word = No Sword = No Power = Defeated Life
OR
Got the Word = Got the Sword = Got Power = Victorious Life

Let's agree: Father, help me to hide Your Word in my heart. Let it guard me from: selfishness, meanness, doubt, impatience, sexual sin, lying, gossip and every other transgression. My desire is not to just memorize

Your Word, but realize the true power in it by radically living it day by day. Thank you Lord, AMEN!

Dream Awake

"We must quickly carry out the tasks assigned us by the One who sent us. The night is coming, and then no one can work." (John 9:4)

And...

"How do you know what your life will be like tomorrow? Your life is like the morning fog—it's here a little while, then it's gone." (James 4:14)

"Some people dream of great accomplishments, while others stay awake and do them." (Constance Newman, Former U.S. Assistant Secretary of State for African Affairs)

Do you have a dream? A goal that you set long ago and just haven't gotten around to pursuing it? Wake up! Begin the work. Don't let sleep slip up on you and relegate your dream to a good idea without hope of fulfillment. Start creating the roadmap for its development today. It's up to you...you can do it! So wake up my sister, my brother...get to work. Your work will make a difference, not only in your life, but in the life of someone in need.

Let's agree: Thank You for the wakeup call today Father. I am awake and ready to begin my work today! Bless the labor of my hands, the direction of my feet, and the motives of my heart. Let the result of my efforts bless others, but also Lord, let it bless me. In Jesus' Name, Amen.

Reckless Drivers

"The Lord is my shepherd; I have all that I need. He lets me rest in green meadows; He leads me beside peaceful streams. He renews my strength. He guides me along right paths, bringing honor to His name." (Psalm 23:1-3)

Who's going to be in the driver's seat this upcoming weekend? You or God? Why not let Him drive? If you do, you will get through it in one emotional piece, If you do not, you just might end up in pieces after you have collided with a selfish loved one or some other person who is too self-absorbed to care about anybody else. You know, people like the relative who only calls when they need something, the spouse who takes you for granted, a rebellious child, or the friend who endlessly talks and never listens. This weekend let God drive, so when you cross paths with these people you won't let them wreck your time of rest.

Let's agree: Thank you Lord for this weekend's time of relaxation. I look to You to guide me in paths of peace. Put Your Word in my mouth, so I can safely travel the treacherous verbal highways and byways of life. In Jesus' Name, Amen!

Do You!

"But you are a chosen people, a royal priesthood, a holy nation, God's special possession, that you may declare the praises of him who called you out of darkness into his wonderful light." (1 Peter 2:9 NIV)

"Do you!" This is an invitation to let your best *you* shine; not to become self-absorbed, but self-respecting. I am encouraging you to respect yourself enough not to allow someone else to use you; love yourself enough not to allow someone else to abuse you; and believe in yourself enough not to let others discourage you. "Do you!" Be the MAN or the WOMAN that God designed you to be. Don't be afraid of what others will think; if you believe God is behind you, don't worry about anyone else's position. God has a plan for you and the only one who can cancel it is you. If you become a puppet for people you will never fulfill God's plan for your life, because there will ALWAYS be someone who is more than willing to take the pin of cynicism and burst your balloon. God created you for greatness, it does not matter if that means living in the White House or being a great mom or dad in your house. You have the potential to be the person who makes a life-changing difference in the lives of others; don't exchange the plan of God for the plan of someone else. Christians are not supposed to fit in with the crowd... "Do you!"

Let's agree: Father, thank You for this word today. So often I am tempted to be a chameleon, changing into whatever the people around me want me to be. Give me strength to overcome "fit-in"ism. Help me to courageously be on assignment, doing and being what You have planned for *me*. I love You Lord. Amen!

Deliverance

"For you have delivered me from death and my feet from stumbling, that I may walk before God in the light of life." (Psalm 56:13 NIV)

The children of Israel wandered in the wilderness forty long years, looking to be delivered, yet not ready for the place God desired to deliver them to. In order to be delivered you are not simply delivered from something, you are delivered to something; you are not just taken from some place, you are delivered to a new place. Are you praying for God's deliverance? If so, ask yourself if you are ready to be delivered to a new place. Are you ready to really leave the mess behind or will you keep looking back like Lot's wife in Genesis 19:24-26? Perhaps you are even tempted to *go* back (Proverbs 26:11) to indulge in the same damaging behavior in which you were previously involved. To truly be delivered, you must let go of that somebody or something that feels good to you, but is not good for you. Realize it may just be "familiarity" that causes you to cling to them/it, and everything familiar is not good. The wilderness had become familiar to the Israelites, but it was not good. Drugs become familiar to the addict, but they are not good. Abuse becomes familiar to the abused, but it is not good. Decide you want a new normal. Let God completely DELIVER you! Go from addicted to drugs, to addicted to Christ; from being overweight due to overeating, to a spiritual heavy weight due to fasting; from out of control anger, to self-control; from an "easy" date, to a desirable date. What is it that you need to be delivered from? Release your grip on it and God WILL deliver you to a better place.

Let's agree: Dear Father, forgive me and help me to forgive myself for staying in this mess so long. I can't explain it; I guess I just lost sight of me and Your best for me. I consciously let go of the people and things that keep me bound, the familiar bad things that the devil uses to tempt me to stay captive. DELIVER me today dear God. Amen.

Feel Bound?

"There is no fear in love. But perfect love drives out fear, because fear has to do with punishment. The one who fears is not made perfect in love. Whoever claims to love God yet hates a brother or sister is a liar. For whoever does not love their brother and sister, whom they have seen, cannot love God, whom they have not seen. And He has given us this command: Anyone who loves God must also love their brother and sister." (1 John 4:18, 20-21)

Animals in the zoo are in habitats, but not their *natural* habitat. Since they are caged in, they can only go so far; in their God-given habitat, they move freely limited only by their knowledge of necessity and safety. The zoo provides an artificial (fake masquerading as real) environment; the real habitat offers much more. Israel experienced years in slavery in Egypt and years in exile, living outside of their natural, God-given (earthly) home. Why? A number of reasons, but a couple of the reasons were the paranoid fears of others and their own disobedience. Things have not changed. The fears of the paranoid still hold people bound in an artificial existence. The wealthy fear anyone who is not, believing they are conspiring to take their wealth. African Americans fear Caucasians believing they all want a return to slavery. Caucasians fear African Americans believing there isn't enough success for us all. Americans fear Hispanics believing all of them are illegally in this country. Educated folk fear the uneducated believing they are holding back the progress of America. Religious people fear other religious people believing another faith will somehow minimize theirs. Let me stop here and say...God is God and there is none other. There is no reason to fear other religions, what Christians should do is pray for the lost, wherever they are found. Truth is, some of them are sitting in worship with us on Sunday mornings. So what am I saying? I am saying fear binds us and separates us from our natural environment of love, peace, joy, and kindness. It binds and separates us. God created ALL of us from 2 people, Adam and Eve. He gave the earth to ALL of us as a temporary home to live and love one another. Let's make an effort to love one another as authentic family...not putting yourself in truly dangerous places, but giving one another a chance. Most of the time, that's all a person is asking for, a chance to live free; limited only by their own ability and determination. How can you personally impact our world in this area? One, by asking God to help you change your fearful thinking. Two, by demonstrating the change in daily life. Three, influence friends and family to do the same. And four, pray that others will get a revelation from God and join this transformative love movement. No more artificial environments, let's get real and set the captives free...that includes all of us!

"If we disobey God, as the people of Israel did, we will fall." (Hebrews 4:11b)

Let's agree: Father, there are so many divisions among us that often I don't even feel related to some of my brothers and sisters. We have allowed the adversary to cause us to mistrust and even hate one another. He has erected dividers that block love all over this planet, especially, it seems, in America. We choose not to love based on economic status, physical attributes, and educational achievement, all of which You disregard in relation to eternity. Forgive me for failing to love others as You love them. Make what is important to You important to me Father. In Jesus' Name, Amen.

Beautiful Thoughts

"Do everything without complaining and arguing." (Philippians 2:14)

Today monitor your thoughts and words. Are you a complainer? Do you like to argue? If you discover these are weaknesses for you, don't beat yourself up. Instead ask God for forgiveness, and strength to change. It's a process. Your daily expectation should be to complain and argue less today than you did yesterday. You *really can* do all things through Christ who gives you the strength! (Philippians 4:13)

Let's agree: Father, this is a beautiful day You have given me. Help me to preserve its beauty with beautiful thoughts, beautiful words, and beautiful behavior. Forgive me for my past complaining and arguing. Help me to add to and not subtract from the beautiful days of my life. Change my negative thinking into positive thinking. I confess my victory over negativity. I have the victory! For I am an overcomer in Christ Jesus my Lord! Amen!

No Peddlers Allowed!

"Submit to God. Resist the devil and he will flee from you!" (James 4:7)

Growing up in a small town, it was not unusual for salespeople to just show up and try to sell random products. Therefore, we had a little medal sign posted on our door "No Peddlers". It meant that Mom didn't want strange people approaching us trying to sell things that we did not need. We did not have a lot of money, so what we did have was not going to be spent foolishly. The sign was effective. I do not remember any encounters with random salesmen. My mother knew that there were people in the world who would try to take advantage of us, so she sent a preemptive message. The message was clear, "We are not buying what you are selling...period!" Some of us need to put a "No Peddlers" sign on our homes. The devil has peddled his lies at your house far too long, its time you stop buying. Stop buying his lie that your life is a dead-end and won't get any better; the lie that your children will never succeed; the lie that peer pressure is stronger in your child's life than your prayers; the lie that you will never change, never be free; the lie that you cannot leave your abuser; the lie that you will never find another job; the lie that you will not be healed; the lie that God does not care; the lie that there is no heaven or hell; the lie that you have no reason to live; the lie that suicide is better than life; the lie that dynamic and spontaneous praise is embarrassing; the lie that you are only a body, so if you lose some of its parts you are not fully you; the lie that our God's power has limits, etcetera, etcetera. The enemy's lies are endless! So, hang out a "No Peddlers" sign on your home, let your children know what it means so they too can have power to reject the devil's lies. No thanks devil, we are not interested in what you are selling! Why? Because God is our sole supply! We get everything we need from Him.

Let's agree: Heavenly Father, thank You for the power You give to me and my family to resist the devil's lies. Keep us alert and vigilant to his attacks. I confess now that he is a defeated foe! Father, I invite You into my home to dwell with us always. In Jesus' Name, Amen.

Smiling Through Your Troubles

"A glad heart makes a happy face; a broken heart crushes the spirit. For the despondent, every day brings trouble; for the happy heart, life is a continual feast." (Proverbs 15:13, 15)

Get these two verses deep in your heart! They are God's personal invitation to enjoy your life! Sometimes our tests can cloud our sunny days, but God said there will always be tests. They are an intentional part of living...not dying. The reality is that there are no tests for the dead, their tests are over. So, do not let tests bring you down! They are a terrific indicator that you are still alive! Today take a deep breath and count your blessings; there is someone somewhere that is dealing with more issues with fewer resources. You have every reason to smile! Not because you are going through difficulty, but because God is not allowing you to go through it alone. He is with you, walking beside you, moving all the obstacles that you cannot handle. Today *is* a good day! Smile, laugh, and live life to the fullest!

Let's agree: Father, too often I allow my tests to break my heart and crush my spirit. I am left feeling despondent always waiting for the next heartbreak, the next disaster. Day after day I awake only to spend the next fourteen to fifteen hours anticipating imagined troubles. Well, today Father, I choose to break free of my misery. I choose to believe You! Even when troubles come they *will* work together for my good! I believe that nothing will show up in my day that I cannot handle! I also believe that every day is a beautiful miracle in which You show me unconditional love. Each day You offer to me boundless joy and hope eternal. Nudge me today Lord and show me Your awesome glory in the sky above, in the trees below, and in the life I've been given. Today I declare in the Powerful Name of Jesus that my life is a continual feast!!! Amen!

Combatting The Darkness

"Casting down imaginations and arguments and every high thing that exalts itself against the knowledge of God, bringing every thought into captivity to the obedience of Christ." (2 Corinthians 10:5)

The power in knowing the Word of God is the ability to combat the darkness of satan's lies with the Light of God's Truth! When darkness comes into your life, go to the Word and speak (read) it out loud in faith over your situation. It's like flipping on the Light switch. When the light enters, darkness flees! Even if you must still deal with the reality of the facts, you will deal with them much better in the Light. Turn on the Light in your life today! Reach for the Word of God, believe the Word of God, and radically live the Word of God! Then, reach out to those who are still stumbling in darkness and point them to the Light switch too.

Let's agree: Father, I choose to walk with You today...all day. I have already received multiple invitations from the enemy to walk in darkness with the spirit of fear, doubt, hate, self- pity, low self-esteem and unforgiveness. The spirit of giving up has made its daily trek across my mind. But today Father, I cast them all down and follow You. Before I go any further in this day, I flip on the Light in my life and reach for Your Word. Today I choose to walk with the Spirit of love, power, and a sound mind. Thank You Lord God for the gift of today, I receive it with joy! I love You. Amen!

The Price Of Acceptance

"If you become wise, you will be the one to benefit. If you scorn wisdom, you will be the one to suffer." (Proverbs 9:12)

Acceptance. Everyone wants it, but what price are you willing to pay for it? Are you willing to pay with your self-esteem, your bank account, your children, your job, your marriage?... You may be thinking "Oh, I would never put anything before my children." But you bring "un-vetted" people around them and behave "un-parental" in front of them. You say, "I wouldn't let someone tear me down." But you constantly let your "special" someone treat you like you were born brainless, yelling at you and demanding from you what you know you should not give. You say you would never be the person who bank rolls someone who is not committed to the relationship...for real (wedding date set and a ring on it). But you give away your hard-earned money every month to pay someone else's bills. Sometimes we are even tempted to put our marriage on the table as the price for acceptance. Have you seen Tyler Perry's "A Family that Preys together?" Our sister offered up a good spouse for a sleazy, no good hound dog. How sad. But if we do not diligently guard our hearts, we can make the same choice. (Proverbs 4:23) The trick is that your temptation may not be sleazy, they may be clean-cut, even another Christian. Brothers, just because she goes to God's house on Sunday does not mean God lives in her house Monday – Saturday. Sisters just because you see him on the back pew, even on the front pew, don't mean his heart is pure. It doesn't mean he's your "love connection". Enough said? We all want to be accepted, but we must not value acceptance above obedience to God. Any relationship that diminishes your relationship with God must itself be diminished.

Let's agree: Dear Lord, heal my heart where it is broken. Strengthen me where I am weak. Father, You are the vine and I am the branch, let my connection with You be enough. Enough to keep me from seeking the approval of people whose lives You do not approve. In Jesus' Name, AMEN!

Grace

"For while the Law was given through Moses, grace (unearned, undeserved favor and spiritual blessing) and truth came through Jesus Christ." (John 1:17)

The next time you visit someone in the hospital ask yourself the question "why are you the visitor and not the patient?" The next time you see an accident in morning or evening traffic ask yourself "why did I arrive without incident?" The answer is Grace. All the near misses, the "should have beens," but wasn'ts. The times you KNOW you should have suffered lost, but didn't. Grace. Grace is getting what you don't deserve. It overrules law. Grace is waking up in the morning and understanding you really had nothing to do with it. Grace is making it to the gas station when you knew you should have run out of gas several miles back. Grace is getting the job, when you know you didn't have the best interview. Grace, it denies us the credit for works. "And since it is through God's kindness, then it is not by our good works. For in that case, God's grace would not be what it really is—free and undeserved." (Romans 11:6)

Let's agree: Thank You Father for Your unmerited favor that covers me all day long and watches over me at night. Thank you for the grace that encourages, saves, and heals. Help me to pass on to others the grace You give to me. In Jesus' Indescribable Name, Amen!

Love And Respect

"If you can't control yourselves, you should go ahead and marry. It's better to marry than to burn with lust." (1 Corinthians 7:9). Furthermore, "He who finds a wife finds a good thing, and obtains favor from the Lord." (Proverbs 18:22)

This is God's instruction for both potential husbands and wives. Men, if you are unable to live celibate lives, God gives you no other option than to find a good woman and marry her. Any other option is contrived by man and is not pleasing to God. Other options, like living with her, but not living for her falls short of God's standard of commitment for human intimate relationships. The option of receiving the privilege of marriage (sex) without marrying treads upon the honor of the woman and the heart of God. Why? Because it dishonors His love of marriage, the gift that He has given to us that chases away loneliness and meets many of our needs. Enticing us to engage in unrestricted sexual activity is the enemy's attempt to reduce the only relationship that reflects the intimacy of Christ and the church to a formality. Marriage is far more than a piece of paper. It is a covenant a man and a woman make *with* God to love and care for one another exclusively for the remainder of their lives. For something to be so precious to God, surely it compels us to elevate it in our hearts as well. Sisters, your part is two-fold. First, stop looking for "him"...it does nothing but frustrate and discourage you when you don't find "him". When we do go looking and find a man, often he is not the one God planned for us.

How do we know he's not the one? Because he does not love us like Christ loves the church. I know the world says "This is the 21st Century, women can look too". But has God's Word changed? Instead of using your energy "looking", spend it "becoming" the good thing that our brothers are looking for.

"Each man must love his wife as he loves himself, and the wife must respect her husband." (Ephesians 5:33)

Brothers, let's agree: Father, thank you for the blessing of marriage and all the gifts that come with it. Help me to honor marriage and love it as You love it. I desire to marry, so help me to find MY good thing, don't let me choose based solely on what I see, but by what I hear from You and her. Teach me to love my future wife as You love the church and gave Your life for it. Let my "finding" journey be enjoyable, enlightening, and pleasing in Your sight dear Lord. Amen!

Sisters, let's agree: Father, thank you for the blessing of marriage and all the gifts that come with it. Help me to honor marriage and love it as You love it. I desire to marry, so help me to become a treasure, a good thing. Do not let me spend my time looking when You said I would be found. But don't let me accept just anyone; help me not to choose based solely on what I see, but by what I hear from You and him. Teach me to love, respect and admire my future husband. Let my "becoming" process be enjoyable, enlightening, and pleasing in Your sight dear Lord. Amen!

Knowledge Is Power!

"A wise person is hungry for knowledge, while the fool feeds on trash." (Proverbs 15:14)

Television has taken the place of books. Video games have taken the place of natural exploration. Belligerent rhythmic shouting has replaced meaningful musical expression. Fighting has taken the place of talking. Gridlock has taken the place of diplomacy. Foolishness prances around pretending to be wisdom. Hypocrisy disguises itself as honesty. Hate says its compassion. Greed make-believes it's generosity. And the rich are mythical allies of the poor. Did you catch the transition from a failure to get knowledge to subject to believe anything? It's subtle. It's also subtle in life. If we fail to educate ourselves we can be duped into believing a lie is the truth. You are a step ahead of the majority of Americans because you are actually reading! This week encourage someone else to do the same. The maxim has not changed, knowledge is still power!

Let's agree: Father, teach me Your ways. Teach me what I need to know, so I can become who I need to become. I want to be a powerful tool in Your hands, Lord. Open my mind to math, science, finances, and politics. Just like You taught our early ancestors to develop earth's first written language, mathematics, science, medicine, literature, and so much more, teach me. In Jesus' Matchless Name, Amen!

Focused On Forgiveness

"If you forgive those who sin against you, your heavenly Father will forgive you. But if you refuse to forgive others, your Father will not forgive your sins." (Matthew 6:14-15)

"Make allowance for each other's faults, and forgive anyone who offends you. Remember, the Lord forgave you, so you must forgive others." (Colossians 3:13)

"Jesus said, 'Father, forgive them, for they don't know what they are doing.' And the soldiers gambled for his clothes by throwing dice." (Luke 23:34)

Forgiveness. It is an amazing concept, and the amazement increases as the enormity of the forgiven offense increases. I find it interesting, however, that God does not dwell on the particular offense or the feelings of the offended person. Instead, He zooms in on the offender and their need of forgiveness. As Jesus hung on the cross, He was not focused on His own pain or the fact that the people who were hurting Him now added insult to injury by gambling over His garments in front of Him. No, instead He responded according to their need, not His pain. He forgave them. This is hard for us to do when someone we love has deeply hurt us. But with the help of the Holy Spirit we must learn. An important key in forgiveness is not confusing the lingering pain of the wound with your feelings about the one who wounded you. Forgiveness does not mean the pain of the offense immediately goes away. Recovery after emotional wounds is much like recovery after physical wounds, it will take time.

Let's agree: Father, thank You for the example of Jesus. Through Him I learn to forgive not based upon my feelings of pain, but upon the offender's need to be forgiven. Help me to forgive quickly, so the devil does not have a chance to plant the seed of bitterness in my heart. Lord, You have forgiven me so many times. Help me to do the same for others. I love You Father. In Jesus' Name, Amen.

Deadly Comparisons

"Pay careful attention to your own work, for then you will get the satisfaction of a job well done, and you won't need to compare yourself to anyone else." (Galatians 6:4)

Comparing kills! It kills hopes and dreams. It kills motivation and drive. It can even kill marriages, working relationships, and friendships. Take the pressure off of yourself by staying away from comparisons. You were wonderfully and fearfully made; there is no one on earth who can beat you being you! So relax and be satisfied with doing YOUR best!

Let's agree: Father, You have poured excellence into me, yet it is so tempting to compare my performance and progress in life with others. Truth is, there will always be someone who has more, performs better, and is more attractive. But it is also true that there will always be someone who has less, does not perform as well, and is less attractive. Help me to realize that comparing adds nothing to my life, it steals from it. Strengthen my resolve to pay careful attention to my own work, so I will be satisfied with a job well done and not feel the need to compare myself to anyone else. Give me the grace and courage to always do my best! Thank You Father. In Jesus' Name, Amen!

Be Bold

People who wink at wrong cause trouble, but a bold reproof promotes peace. (Proverbs 10:10)

I know this is a tough Word, but think about the little things we regularly let slip by without a word of objection. Consider this...we laugh at inappropriate jokes, encourage the use of bad language, excuse racist comments, hang around listening to gossip, and giggling at cutting words which hurt the feelings of others.....much of the time because we are glad we're not the target. The list goes on. Sometimes we just need to not laugh or walk away. And when God prompts us, we need to speak up for right.

Let's agree: Father, it is difficult to be the one who tells the truth about bad behavior. So much is "acceptable" in our world. People often call right wrong and wrong right. When You set me up to be the voice of truth give me the courage to speak and the wisdom to speak with love. Help me to remember that I make mistakes too and will also need loving reproof in the future. Thank You Father for teaching me to promote peace through the loving correction of others. Amen.

Fear

"They were all terrified when they saw him. But Jesus spoke to them at once. "Don't be afraid," he said. "Take courage! I am here! " (Mark 6:50)

Fear is a part of everyone's life. It's part of being human. The only way to have no fear is to have all power. We do not, so we experience fear of the unknown. Just think about it, how many "unknowns" have you worried and bound with fear right now? You try to pretend you have not a worry in the world when in reality you wrestle with fear constantly. Fear of financial devastation, fear of failure, fear of divorce, fear of disease, fear of hair loss, fear of impotency, fear of inadequacy, the list goes on. How do we get it all under control? By remembering what Jesus said: "Don't be afraid. Take courage! I am here! " So, whatever you are dealing with today, be strong and courageous! Jesus is with you! He will protect you, guide you, and help you if you let Him.

Let's agree: Father, the enemy is cunning in his methods of getting me upset and wrapped around the axle. Sometimes he attacks so quickly that I am tossed off of my spiritual feet before I even know what happened; unexpected situations that pop up and cause me to fear the outcome. When these things happen Father, help me not to become paralyzed with fear, but instead to immediately look to You, remembering You are with me. Trials and tribulations are a part of life, but You promise to walk with me THROUGH them all! Lord, instead of succumbing to the paralysis of fear, give me strength to sing Your praises! I declare fear will no longer paralyze my faith, my prayers, or my praise! When fear attacks I fight back in the Mighty Name of Jesus! Amen!

Lazy People

Lazy people irritate their employers, like vinegar to the teeth or smoke in the eyes. (Proverbs 10:26)

Do you know someone who goes to work, but does not work? However, they will be the first one to tell you how good God is and quote some Scripture. This presents a distorted picture of a Christian, because God's goodness and His Word should translate to a diligent employee. Why? Because our Father has told us to do all our work as though we were working for Him. (Colossians 3:23) In reality God is your supervisor, so give Him a reason to give you a bonus! We are the King's kids and we need to reflect Him in all we do. So, let's go to work....for real.

Let's agree: Father, help me to remember that I represent You at work just as I represent You in a place of worship on Saturday or Sunday morning. Today, I must admit that sometimes I do not give my best effort; I get distracted or frustrated. Forgive me Lord. Help me to overcome half-hearted effort and fear of failure. I declare right now that moving forward my work will be excellent; reflecting the excellence in You! Thanks for not giving up on me Father. I love You, Amen.

Something For Nothing

"Whatever you give is acceptable if you give it eagerly. And give according to what you have, not what you don't have." (2 Corinthians 8:12)

"You should remember the words of the Lord Jesus: 'It is more blessed to give than to receive.' " (Acts 20:35)

Some folks are professional moochers, always looking to get something for nothing. This is true both in the natural and spiritual. There are people who have mooched so long in the natural that this attitude has carried over into their relationship with God. They are always looking to be blessed by God, but never want to give Him anything…time, service, or obedience. They just hang around the fringes of Christianity so when their worldly, selfish ways fail they can feel entitled to be bailed out of their mess by God. They live a life of selective memory, only remembering God's promises of blessings, but forgetful when it comes to His command for obedience. They seek His grace and forgiveness, deliverance and power. However, they flee God's commands to sacrifice their time and energy. They make excuses for not using their gifts and talents to give Him glory. So, if you have been a moocher, natural or spiritual, change the script of your life and begin looking for ways to give instead of take. Remember, the greatest blessing is in giving, not taking.

Let's agree: Father, thank You for giving so graciously to me. Place inside of me the same generous spirit. Teach me to give of my love, my time, my knowledge, my understanding, my wisdom, my patience, and my finances. Father, help me to be a good steward of all that You have given to me. In the Mighty Name of Jesus, Amen!

Idle Living

"Yet we hear that some of you are living idle lives, refusing to work and meddling in other people's business. We command such people and urge them in the name of the Lord Jesus Christ to settle down and work to earn their own living." (2 Thessalonians 3:11- 12)

Been just hanging out? Chillin'? Letting someone else work and take care of you although you are grown enough to take care of yourself? Stop! It's time to settle down, grow up and earn your own way. What's your plan? And what is your plan to implement your plan? Planning is great, but if the plan remains just a plan and never becomes a project, it will never become a reality. So, stop hanging out. It leads to boredom which leads to meddling in other people's business. Like my Granny used to say, "Idleness is the devil's workshop!" If you do not have a healthy life plan, create one; and do not forget to include the roadmap to making it a reality. The ability to achieve greatness is inside of you! Start using it today!

Let's agree: Father, thank You for the potential You have given me. Help me to stop wasting the minutes, hours, and days of my life in idleness. Guide me to my niche, that something that I will find great joy in doing. Direct me to the right people and places at the right time. Open the doors of opportunity before me; and forgive me for my delay on my journey toward destiny. Redeem the time for me, Father. In Jesus' Name, Amen!

Shine!

"You are the light of the world—like a city on a hilltop that cannot be hidden. No one lights a lamp and then puts it under a basket. Instead, a lamp is placed on a stand, where it gives light to everyone in the house. In the same way, let your good deeds shine out for all to see, so that everyone will praise your heavenly Father." (Matthew 5:14-16)

Every day is a spiritual battle. Whether you realize it or not when you lie down at night you are in battle and when you wake up in the morning you are in battle. Our enemy is relentless and determined, therefore, we must be also! We fight the devil not for eternal victory; that fight has already been won on Calvary's cross. We fight for a daily victory that serves as a light to unbelievers. It reminds me of the Motel 6 motto, "We'll leave the light on for you." When Jesus ascended back to heaven He told the unsaved, "I'll leave the Light on for you." We are that Light, *Christ living inside of us!* The battle still rages for souls and as believers, we must continue to shine brightly in this dark world! It's hard for the devil to fight when he is blinded by the Light. So, let's shine brightly in our homes, at our jobs, in the classroom and in the boardroom! Game on!!! Devil you lose!

Let's agree: Father, You have left Your Light in me and placed me in a place for others to see. Forgive me for harboring secret sins that dim my Light. I want to be a radiant spiritual floodlight directing unbelievers to safe harbor in You. Shine brightly through me today Lord! In Jesus' Holy Name, Amen!

Is The Grass Really Greener....Over There?

"But as for me, I almost lost my footing. My feet were slipping, and I was almost gone. For I envied the proud when I saw them prosper despite their wickedness. They seem to live such painless lives; their bodies are so healthy and strong. They don't have troubles like other people; they're not plagued with problems like everyone else. They wear pride like a jeweled necklace and clothe themselves with cruelty. These fat cats have everything their hearts could ever wish for! Did I keep my heart pure for nothing? Did I keep myself innocent for no reason? Then I went into your sanctuary, O God, and I finally understood the destiny of the wicked. Truly, you put them on a slippery path and send them sliding over the cliff to destruction. Then I realized that my heart was bitter, and I was all torn up inside." (Psalms 73:2-7, 13, 17, 18, 21)

When you begin to focus on the lives of others instead of focusing on your own life, you can experience "the grass is greener" syndrome. From the outside looking in you think someone else's life is perfect while yours is a constant struggle. But appearances can be deceptive and you never know what price is being paid for that "appearance." Some of these people silently endure domestic abuse, while others suffer from depression and loneliness. Some people have even sold their souls to the devil, turning their back on all things holy, to gain fame and riches. That is a mighty high price to pay for a temporary living arrangement. Temporary because heaven and earth shall pass away, and life is but a vapor.

As the old song says, "only what we do for Christ will last!" Cars won't, houses won't, golf clubs, jet skis, and yachts won't, clothes, purses and shoes won't, and neither will diamonds, gold, or cash. So don't get bitter about what you do not have in this world, get excited about what you have in Christ!

Let's agree: Father, forgive me for coveting the lives of others. Help me to stay focused on what You are doing in my life. It is not always easy, You never promised it would be. But You did promise to be with me through life's journey, and You did promise an eternal home in a place where the streets are paved with gold. In that place I won't cry anymore; I'll never be lonely or left out. In that place there will be no more upper class, middle class, or lower class, just worshippers of the King! But until then Lord, I will find sanctuary in You! In Your name Jesus, Amen!

My Garden Of Gethsemane

"I pray that your hearts will be flooded with light so that you can understand the confident hope he has given to those he called—his holy people who are his rich and glorious inheritance." (Ephesians 1:18)

There are people; maybe it is you, who are exhausted from giving what they consider their best and getting so little in return. Know this, there are times that all of us feel like we cannot go on. The devil wants us to believe trials and tribulations come because of some sin or irresponsibility on our part. Sometimes we do cause our own pain, but not always. There are times we are allowed to struggle so we can gain strength. In the future, when the devil tries to make you feel bad about yourself because of your struggles, hold your head up and thank God because you will get the last laugh! Just know that after this season of pain, you will be harder for the enemy to deal with! So, don't let the devil take you emotionally under, let God take you through! Through the doubt, worry, and tears. Our heavenly Father has given to all of His children the confident hope in Him necessary for overcoming every situation. It is up to us to release our cares to Him in prayer. What does your prayer life look like? Is it consistent? Is it personal or an exercise of habit? Remember how Jesus labored in prayer in the Garden of Gethsemane? *(Mark 14:32-36 NIV)* Meet Jesus in your own Garden of Gethsemane. Carry your burdens to Him and leave them there. If you do, you will leave the Garden with renewed strength to deal with life's challenges.

Let's agree: Dear Father, though my trials seem heavy and endless, I know that You have not and will not allow more than I can bear. Lord, I bring with me today the burdens that I have tried to carry. I got so involved in life that I reverted back to my old way of attempting to do things on my own. Well, right now heavenly Father, I am giving them back to You. Thank You for this Garden experience. I leave lighter and with confident hope that my best days are yet before me! In the Name of Your risen Son, Jesus, Amen!!!

The Privilege Of Prayer

"Therefore confess your sins to each other and pray for each other so that you may be healed. The prayer of a righteous person is powerful and effective." (James 5:16 NIV)

For Christians, prayer is not only a major assignment, it's a privilege. Have you ever had a problem staying awake when it was time to pray? I have! The devil knows great power flows from fervent effectual prayers, so he works overtime to prevent focused, purposeful, and faith-filled prayer. This is why we cannot be discouraged in praying. It doesn't matter if you fall asleep. Fall asleep with "Jesus" on your lips! If you have a challenging day ahead or had a challenging day today and you are finding it difficult to focus in your prayers, just focus on His name, Jesus! If worry tries to invade the peace of your prayer, cast your cares on Him! He will take your burdens and release peace to defeat your worry! Don't let the devil trick you out of your privilege of prayer! Hold tight to it! It is your divine assignment!

Let's agree: Father, what a privilege it is to speak with You throughout my day. Talking to You brings me peace and confidence. Peace in that nothing that happens today is beyond Your ability to handle and confidence in the gifts and talents You have given to me. As I journey through each day, may Your glory shine through me. Let my attitude be evidence of time spent with You, not combative, cruel, or critical; instead, patient, kind, and joyful. Let *my* smile testify of Your unquestionable goodness. May the beauty of Your love make today a beautiful day in my life Father. In Jesus' Name, Amen!

Overcoming Evil

"Don't let evil conquer you, but conquer evil by doing good." (Romans 12:21)

February is Black History Month in our nation. Some may question the necessity of this designation. But when a nation has such a deep historical wound, it demands special attention to ensure infection does not set in causing a setback in healing. Our nation has made wonderful strides in the area of racial equality, however, there is much left to be done. There is new ground to be gained and old ground that has been lost that needs to be re-gained. The question that each of us should consider today is "What does my personal commitment to Christ compel me to do to improve race relations in America?" It can be as simple as smiling at someone or inviting them to join you for lunch. Refuse to be a part of the problem, someone that perpetuates destructive and unfounded stereotypes about groups of people, instead of understanding and judging one individual at a time. God has said, "Don't let evil conquer you, but conquer evil by doing good." This means you must stop feeding any attitude or behavior that you do not want to keep alive in your life. If you do not want to be racially biased, then do not feed racially biased thoughts. Cut them off. TV does not help much with positive racial thinking. As a matter of fact, it consistently presents negative images that promote division. This being the case, consider reducing TV time for you and your family. By doing so you will refuse to be programmed by network programing (TV programs). *Don't feed any thoughts you don't want manifested in your behavior. If it is in you, when you're squeezed, it will come out.*

Let's agree: Father, help me to realize that what we call diversity was Your intentional act of creativity. When You created humanity and said "It is good" You were not looking at one moment in time, but ALL moments in time. In that moment, You saw ALL of us, every person to ever live! The black, white, brown, yellow, red and every shade in between were in Your loving, parental view that day. Help me to accept everyone I meet for who they are...Your child. Today I resolve to overcome evil with good! In Jesus' Name, Amen!

Born To Fly

"When someone has been given much, much will be required in return; and when someone has been entrusted with much, even more will be required." (Luke 12:48b)

Have you noticed that larger aircraft need longer runways to take off? This is due to the fact that they must build up power to become airborne. Smaller aircraft can use shorter runways or use less of the long runway because their taxiing distance is shorter. Let's relate this to life. When you keep experiencing challenges when everyone else seems to be receiving their breakthrough just remember to whom much is given much is required. It may take you longer to take off, but your flight will be more amazing because you will reach higher altitudes! People will see you fly and wonder how it is possible that someone who has been through so much can fly so high! You may be going through a lot right now, but just remember your reward will be great! So buckle up and keep taxiing! You will soon have the power to takeoff and sore!

Let's agree: Father, sometimes my load feels too heavy for me to takeoff. I question whether I am built to fly at all since my efforts to succeed keep failing. But You said if I wait on You, I will mount up on wings as eagles! I *will* fly! You have given me the ability. Father, though my runway is long, I know my flight will give You great glory. I declare today that these current trials will soon be the wind beneath my wings instead of the weight that holds me down. In the meantime Lord, help me to keep my head up as I travel the runway of life. Help me to gain momentum with every step I take! Give me the power to takeoff and soar! In Jesus' Holy Name, Amen!

Gifted And Grateful

"There are different kinds of gifts, but the same Spirit distributes them." (1 Corinthians 12:4 NIV)

Here's an empowering concept "humble confidence." This means having unwavering confidence in the gifts God has placed in you, yet maintaining a humble heart knowing without God you can do nothing! It means you can be excellent in whatever you do. You can operate with assurance! Humble confidence means you can handle success without getting the big head. It translates into you enjoying the achievement, but giving God the glory. So go ahead and celebrate your successes, just remember the power, intelligence, and ability you used to gain those successes came directly from God!

Let's agree: Father, thank You for the gifts You have given to me. Help me to develop them and use them responsibly to edify the Church and to be a blessing wherever I am. Guard my heart from arrogance. Give me the power to maintain a humble spirit even when I experience great triumphs. For truly there are different kinds of gifts, but the same Spirit...Your Spirit, who distributes them all. In Jesus' Incomparable Name, Amen!

No Place To Hide

"I can never escape from your Spirit! I can never get away from your presence! If I go up to heaven, you are there; if I go down to the grave, you are there. If I ride the wings of the morning, if I dwell by the farthest oceans, even there your hand will guide me, and your strength will support me. I could ask the darkness to hide me and the light around me to become night—but even in darkness I cannot hide from you. To you the night shines as bright as day. Darkness and light are the same to you." (Psalms 139:7-12)

Many of us have settings on our cell phones and iPads that can give people our current location any hour of the day or night. It can identify if we are at home, at the store, in another state, etc. This is a pretty nifty application. If we want our location to be unknown we just disable the setting. This works great with technology, but it does not work at all spiritually. There is nothing we can do to hide from God, but how often do we try? We attempt to hide our spiritual location by disabling our prayer lives. We did not get our prayer answered in the time or the way that we wanted, so we reduce our connectivity to God. We tell ourselves why bother if He's going to do whatever He wants anyway! But as a Christian, isn't that exactly what we want...His will? God knows what is best for you. He knows what you can handle and when you can handle it. So, stop with the pity party. Come out of spiritual hiding and reconnect with God, He knows where you are anyway, no technology required!

Let's agree: Father, forgive me for pouting when I don't get my way. Help me to trust Your timing above my planning. You know what is best for me. You are using every mountain and valley experience for my good. Your plan for my life will far outreach the outer limits of my greatest hopes! Moving forward, I want to trust *You* more than *me*. Help me Lord! In Jesus' Powerful Name, Amen!

New Day, New Normal

"I tell you the truth, anyone who believes in Me will do the same works I have done, and even greater works, because I am going to be with the Father." (John 14:12)

What's going to be *your* new normal today? Step out on faith! Exercise courage! Live with confidence! God is for you! He's more than the world against you! Believe it? Then show it! Live BIG!

B elieving
I n
G od!

When you live BIG you no longer allow yourself to be ridden with worry because you cast all your cares on Him expecting Him to sustain you. (Psalm 55:22) When you live BIG you do not let envy lead you to spend your time tearing down people behind their backs, because you are confident that God has a special plan just for you and it can't be stolen, cancelled, or duplicated. (Jeremiah 29:11) Living BIG means you no longer get caught up dating someone who fails to see your true value, because you are clear on the fact that our God does and He is crazy about you! (John 3:16) Living BIG means being different because you live by a higher standard; being accepted by the popular crowd is no longer a goal, because that standard is far too low. Many people desire to Live Large and they will do almost anything to achieve popularity and wealth. But Living Large doesn't compare with living BIG because Living Large ceases when death enters the scene. When you live BIG death just means you upsize to a mansion in heaven and are freed from the superficial interest of the world. So don't just pursue Living Large, decide to live BIG!

Let's agree: Father, reshape what's normal in my life. I declare today, in the name of Jesus, that I am courageous, confident, and full of faith! From this day forward I use the power You have given me to overcome the adversary on every hand! Greater is He that is in me than He that is in the world! For the rest of my life my spiritual footprint will change lives! It will change MY life forever! I live B-I-Gger today than I did yesterday, believing in You more!!! In Jesus' Powerful Name, Amen!

The Value Of Good Blocking

"A thousand may fall at your side, ten thousand at your right hand, but it will not come near you. For He will command His angels concerning you to guard you in all your ways; they will lift you up in their hands, so that you will not strike your foot against a stone. 'Because He loves me,' says the Lord, 'I will rescue him; I will protect him, for he acknowledges My name.'" (Psalm 91:7, 11, 12, 14 NIV)

Good coverage is priceless. If you watched the 2014 BCS Championship Game between Auburn and Florida State, you witnessed this truth when Florida State's #7 (Whitfield) made a great punt return that resulted in a Florida State touchdown. His run was beautiful and showcased his talent, but it would not have been possible had he not had great blocking by his teammate #9 (Williams). The same is true for Auburn's #21 (Mason) who made a late 4th quarter TD. Ask any football player, they will tell you that getting from one end of the field to the other is so much easier when there is good run coverage. This is also true in life. Running this race that begins at birth and ends at death can be mighty tough without folks who are willing to get out ahead and provide the blocking you need. Though human help is a blessing, there is no better blocker than our heavenly Father. In life there are challenges we must face that sometimes leave bumps and bruises, but the reality is we have no idea how many more debilitating and damaging hits we would endure if our God had not blocked them.

Let's agree: Thank You Father for great run coverage! Because of You, I will keep running this race until I cross life's goal line in victory. On that day I will dance my own victory dance on the streets of gold! I praise You Lord that my life is a spiritual touchdown! I win! In Jesus' Victorious Name, Amen!

Keeping Power

"For in the day of trouble He will keep me safe in His dwelling; He will hide me in the shelter of His sacred tent and set me high upon a rock. Then my head will be exalted above the enemies who surround me; at His sacred tent I will sacrifice with shouts of joy; I will sing and make music to the Lord." (Psalm 27:5, 6 NIV)

God has keeping power! Sometimes the influence of the world seems overwhelming, but God has a proven track record as a Keeper. He kept Lot's family in the midst of Sodom and Gomorrah. He kept Israel in the desert, and He kept Moses in Egypt. He kept David in the midst of wars, Joseph in the midst of famine, and He kept Noah in an epic flood. He kept Daniel in the lion's den and the three Hebrew boys in the fiery furnace. What do you need God to keep you in; financial trouble, relationship trouble, or perhaps employment trouble? Whatever your trouble, God can keep you. His grace and power are more than sufficient to bring you through! So, instead of throwing up your hands in defeat, throw them up in victory!

Let's agree: Father, You said there would be trials and tribulations, times of trouble that threaten to shake my faith. But God I recall how You provided safety for so many others; I believe You will also provide safety for me. You are my shelter in the midst of trouble. You are the lifter of my head. You will bring me through and exalt me high above all my trouble and all the troublemakers. Therefore Father, I will enter Your presence with shouts of joy; I will sing and make music to You. Praises be unto my God! In the Prevailing Name of Jesus, Amen!

An Annoying Assignment

"Be kind and compassionate to one another, forgiving each other, just as in Christ God forgave you." (Ephesians 4:32 NIV)

Have you ever had someone in your life that constantly annoyed you? I have! I truly did not want to be annoyed by them, but their behavior was simply irritating! What do you do?! Here is my suggestion. Accept these two facts and they will make accepting annoying people a little easier. First, remind yourself that the person is likely not annoying you on purpose. Their behavior is triggered by a natural instinct that is shaped by their culture, rearing, and experiences. To them, their behavior is "normal." Second, remember that the personal contact with the individual may not be all about you, but all about them. God may have placed you together to benefit *them*! So, take another look at the connection, you may be on assignment! Pray for enough love, patience, and wisdom to impact the person's life according to God's will.

Let's agree: Father, whew! I can't imagine what You deal with every second of every day. All the different personalities! I have difficulty handling the few human encounters I am responsible for in my lifetime. Help me to remember that when I accepted Jesus as Savior, my life became a tool in Your toolbox that You use to fix broken lives. It is NOT all about me. Use me Lord to heal, direct, and impact this generation for You! In Jesus' Holy Name, Amen!

Due Time

"Humble yourselves under the mighty hand of God, that He may exalt you in due time." (I Peter 5:6 NKJV)

Have you ever felt that your faith worked better on other people's lives than it does on your own? For example, you pray with a friend for a financial blessing and they receive an amazing monetary windfall. Praise God! But you have been praying for a personal financial blessing too, without results. This can be discouraging! But know that God's timing is not the same for everyone. It is like He is the divine director of an orchestra of lives! Just as orchestra members do not all play the same note at the same time, we do not all experience blessings and trials at the same time. But as with the orchestra, we will all have our opportunity to use our gift. So standby; do not stay discouraged. Trust and believe your solo is on the way! Just keep an encouraging spirit and keep praying for yourself and those in need around you. Sooner than you think, God will point to you and it will be your time to be exalted; your time of abundant blessing. So stay humble, wait your turn, and at God's appointed time you will be blessed beyond measure!

Let's agree: Father, even though I do not always understand Your timing, I trust it. Keep me in faith though I am struggling with life. I know that You know what is best for me. I humble myself to Your perfect love, perfect plan, and perfect timing. Help me to keep doing what I can while You are doing what I can't. In Jesus' Exalted Name, Amen!

Offering My Best

"So God created man in His own image; in the image of God He created him; male and female He created them. Then God blessed them." (Genesis 1:27, 28a NKJV)

"Be diligent to present yourself..." (II Timothy 2:15a NKJV)

If you are someone who hides behind the fact, turned excuse, that your spouse should love you for who you are, let me encourage you to consider this. When you go to the grocery store or the mall do you look for the best items or the average items? I would guess you look for and expect the best. I do too! Why then do you expect your spouse to be satisfied with average? I'm not suggesting brothers that you need to look like Morris Chestnut, Antonio Banderas, L.L. Cool J, or Brad Pitt. And sisters I'm certainly not saying we need to be replicas of Hallie Berry, Angelina Jolie, Beyoncé, or Eva Mendes. What I am encouraging you to do is invest in yourself so you are constantly presenting your spouse with your best you, not some dim reflection of who you used to be. Begin to read to expand your mind, exercise and eat right to get physically fit, dress attractively, and maintain good hygiene (head to toe). Finally, it goes without saying that if you are a Christian, you should be seeking God through pray and His Word and growing in your faith. If you are guilty of taking your spouse for granted, surprise them by offering them a better you starting today! I'm praying for your endurance and success!

Let's agree: Father, please forgive me for being a lazy lover. You have given me a wonderful spouse and I have not responded with Your best in me. Please motivate and energize me to do, say, and be what will bless my precious husband/wife. Although I know they are not perfect either, help me to stay focused on improving myself and leave their self-improvement to You. Bless my marriage Lord. Make it more fulfilling for us both. When we are not together, let us long for one another's company. When we think of one another, let the thoughts bring a smile to our faces. When we touch, let it bring reassurance and comfort. Heal my marriage Father. Fill our hearts and our home with Your powerful and enduring LOVE. Please give us another chance Lord. In the Heart-healing and Heart-changing Name of Jesus, Amen!

Friends Indeed

"As iron sharpens iron, so a friend sharpens a friend." (Proverbs 27:17)

What kind of relationships do you have? Are they relationships that make you better? Do an assessment of your friends today; you may have misplaced some friends in the discard pile that need to be in your inner circle. On the other hand, you may have a few folks in your friend files that definitely belong on the curb on big trash pickup day. Life is short, nurture relationships that breathe life into you and discard relationships that do nothing but slow your progress, depress you, and tempt you to sin. Who needs that?! Set yourself free from toxic relationships today! You deserve friends who are friends indeed!

Let's agree: Father, give me wisdom to assess my inner circle and the courage to make needed changes. Do not let fear or dread keep me emotionally handcuffed to deadbeat "friends". I want to enjoy my life with people who enjoy theirs and enhance mine. Give me wonderful friends, Lord, and shape me into a wonderful friend too. In Jesus' Amazing Name, Amen!

Bandwagon Mentality

"Oh, the joys of those who do not follow the advice of the wicked, or stand around with sinners, or join in with mockers." (Psalms 1:1)

As human beings we can get caught up in the "bandwagon mentality." You know, when people go along to get along. It is easier to stick with the crowd than stick out as different. In the 60's, there was a system of racism in place called Jim Crow. This system denied basic rights to Blacks solely due to the shade of their skin. This system not only oppressed Blacks, but it challenged Whites to make a stand for racial equality.....or not. Many found it easier to get on the bandwagon of hatred than to stand on their own two feet and walk with those fighting for freedom. But there were some who did not follow the advice of the wicked, they did not hang out with sinners or join the mockers of justice. They were Whites who risked their lives to stand for Truth. Courtesy of the Southern Poverty Law Center's website, here are some of their names and the sacrifices they made. (www.splcenter.org)

April 7, 1964 · Cleveland, Ohio

Rev. Bruce Klunder was among civil rights activists who protested the building of a segregated school by placing their bodies in the way of construction equipment. Klunder was crushed to death when a bulldozer backed over him.

September 30, 1962 · Oxford, Mississippi

Paul Guihard, a reporter for a French news service, was killed by gunfire from a white mob during protests over the admission of James Meredith to the University of Mississippi.

April 23, 1963 · Attalla, Alabama
William Lewis Moore, a postman from Baltimore, was shot and killed during a one-man march against segregation. Moore had planned to deliver a letter to the governor of Mississippi urging an end to intolerance.

June 21, 1964 · Philadelphia, Mississippi
Andrew Goodman and Michael Henry Schwerner, young civil rights workers, were arrested by a deputy sheriff and then released into the hands of Klansmen who had plotted their murders. They were shot, and their bodies were buried in an earthen dam.

March 11, 1965 · Selma, Alabama
Rev. James Reeb, a Unitarian minister from Boston, was among many white clergymen who joined the Selma marchers after the attack by state troopers at the Edmund Pettus Bridge. Reeb was beaten to death by white men while he walked down a Selma street.

March 25, 1965 · Selma Highway, Alabama
Viola Gregg Liuzzo, a housewife and mother from Detroit, drove alone to Alabama to help with the Selma march after seeing televised reports of the attack at the Edmund Pettus Bridge. She was driving marchers back to Selma from Montgomery when she was shot and killed by a Klansmen in a passing car.

Let's agree: Father, thank You for the strength of those who refused to hide behind their skin. Thank You for their example of integrity and courage. As the unfortunate struggle for racial equality continues, convict Your people in positions of authority to take up the task of ensuring equal opportunities for all people. Lord, let Your spirit move to and fro across our nation correcting the wrongs. Transform racist hearts into loving hearts, erase the wicked plans of the oppressor to perpetuate distrust, and wash away the stain of hate upon our nation. Haters are in the minority, use me to rally the majority to reject the sin of hate and overcome it with a love for all people. In Jesus' Amazing Name, Amen!

Learn Right, Live Right!

"Obey My commands and live! Guard My instructions as you guard your own eyes." (Proverbs 7:2)

One of the dangers of becoming comfortable just coming to “church” on a weekly basis is that we come to believe that it is all that is necessary to live a Christian life. This is far from the truth. God gave us His Word to promote life! As a matter of fact, true life is impossible without the Word, because the Word is the Bread, the sustenance of life. Without it, we become spiritually weak and will eventually live dead lives, physically alive, but spiritually life-less. So, don’t get comfortable with the minimum in Christian service, max out and live what you learn!

Let's agree: Father, thank You for another day of life. Today I ask You to stir Your Word in my heart. Let it rise to the surface of my life and rain blessings into my day. In Jesus' Name, Amen!

Get Motivated!

Regardless of what day of the week it is get motivated! If you feel like you are in a rut, open your heart to God's motivating Word!

"For God is working in you, giving you the desire and the power to do what pleases Him." (Philippians 2:13)

Don't doubt the potential for greatness that our God has planted in your life! Anything that He has planned for you to do, no matter how grand, you can do it! Here's a new mantra to keep you focused on the *greater* God has for you, "Don't be deceived by doubt, be fortified by faith!" You have the power to make a difference in this world, so do it! Dig in and let your preparation propel you forward!

Let's agree: Father, thank You for giving me great potential. Help me to believe in my ability to do great things to enhance the world in which I live. Help me to be positive in my thoughts and conversations about "me". Today I declare out of me mouth that greatness is alive in *me*! My future is blessed, my past is over, and today offers a fresh start on my journey to greatness! I am motivated to do marvelous things in Jesus' Name, Amen!

All Things...Really?!

"For I can do everything through Christ, who gives me strength." (Philippians 4:13)

If this Scripture is familiar to you do not just read it and miss out on the fresh anointing that resides in it. Read it again, this time slowly and thoughtfully. Now think about it for a minute... Christ working in me can close my mouth at the right time, open my eyes to foolishness (mine as well as others), give me wisdom, and help me achieve my dreams. When Christ is working in me mountains are not as high and valleys are not as low. Christ at work in you is the reason you can celebrate tomorrow's victories today!

Let's agree: Father, thank You for Jesus! Thank You for the strength You give me to overcome *every* obstacle. I walk in Your strength today. I not only handle every challenge with grace, I make great strides toward my goals. For I CAN do ALL things THROUGH CHRIST who strengthens me! In Jesus' Name, Amen!

"Why" Matters!

"But I, the Lord, search all hearts and examine secret motives. I give all people their due rewards, according to what their actions deserve." (Jeremiah 17:10)

Do you know people who are driven by personal agendas? I am sure we all do. These are people who will lie to their mother to advance their agenda. All that matters to them is reaching their own personal goals; there is no cap on the cost. They see not problem with being rude, cruel, and destructive if it advances their personal cause. When confronted with their methods and the impact of their decisions on others, these folks always have a “legitimate reason” for their behavior. Since they believe their agenda is a secret, the reasons they give for their poor conduct often mask the real motive for their unkindness. As Christians, we must not deceive ourselves into believing God is unaware of our authentic purposes. He is not! Thus, if you are caught up in a personal agenda that does not have God’s stamp of approval, you need to stop, pray, and listen. You do not want to one day receive the due rewards of actions driven by a bad agenda.

Let's agree: Father, I have not always been driven by the right motives. I have been selfish, proud, and greedy. Today I turn in my personal agenda and reach out to You for Yours. May the rest of my life be built upon the firm foundation of Your word. Guide me to make the right choices for the right reasons, so that one day, I will receive the due rewards for a life motivated by love and characterized by kindness. In Jesus' Name, Amen!

Conquerors!

"No, despite all these things, overwhelming victory is ours through Christ, who loved us." (Romans 8:37)

What does this mean? It means that no matter what the day holds you have already been given the strength necessary to deal with it and come out on top! It means that you can be excited about your future today because the race is rigged...you have the victory! There is no way you can lose with Christ! So go ahead and dream about the finish line. You win!

Let's agree: Father, how excited and grateful I am that You have planned a good ending to the story of my life. Regardless of what each individual chapter may hold, You have written in a happy ending! Even though there are days that I become angry and nights that I shed many tears, none of this changes my ending. My hope is in You. No one but You can promise victory when all appears to be lost. No one but You can assure me of, not just a victory in my trials, but an overwhelming victory! I declare right now that I am more than an overcomer in Christ Jesus, my Lord! Amen!

When Wrong Feels Right

"There is a path before each person that seems right, but it ends in death." (Proverbs 16:25)

Sometimes we translate comfort to "rightness" and discomfort to "wrongness". But the fact is things that are wrong that can "feel" right and things that are right can feel all wrong. This is why it is critical to be intimately connected to our Heavenly Father through His Word and prayer. When you are close to Him, you have no need to depend on feelings, you can hear His voice. Get connected, stay connected, and live a powerful life!

"Many will be purified, cleansed, and refined by these trials. But the wicked will continue in their wickedness, and none of them will understand. Only those who are wise will know what it means." (Daniel 12:10)

Let's agree: Father, I come to You today thanking You for protecting me from bad decisions. Draw me nearer so I can discern right from wrong; not based upon my feelings, but according to Your revealed will in prayer and Scripture. Father, keep my feet and my desires on the path of righteousness. In the Name of Jesus, Amen!

Three Days

"The Lord gave this message to Jonah son of Amittai: "Get up and go to the great city of Nineveh. Announce my judgment against it because I have seen how wicked its people are." But Jonah got up and went in the opposite direction to get away from the Lord. He went down to the port of Joppa, where he found a ship leaving for Tarshish. He bought a ticket and went on board, hoping to escape from the Lord by sailing to Tarshish. But the Lord hurled a powerful wind over the sea, causing a violent storm that threatened to break the ship apart. Now the Lord had arranged for a great fish to swallow Jonah. And Jonah was inside the fish for three days and three nights." (Jonah 1:1-4, 17)

Are you dealing with the Jonah syndrome? No peace because you are resisting the will of God? You know what is right, yet you refuse to obey because it is not what you want? Well, expect a big fish in your future! You can pray now, pray in the fish's belly, or stubbornly languish there in rebellion. Are you in the fish's belly today? How long will you stay? It took Jonah three days. Hopefully it will not take you that long!

"Then Jonah prayed to the Lord his God from inside the fish." (Jonah 2:1)

Let's agree: Father, I have been stubborn and strong-willed insisting on my own way. Please forgive me and lead me back to the way of righteousness. I have spent long enough in the belly of this fish. I do not want to languish here missing out on the joys of life. What You have asked me to do is not what I want...it scares me, angers me, humbles me and I do not want to do it! But Lord I decide right now to do it anyway. You said go, so I go. If I must forgive, I will. If I must give, I will. If I must witness to the one who hurt me, I will. If I must volunteer my time, I will. Whatever You say Lord I am now willing to do. May Your anointing be on my life as it was Jonah's when he finally made it to Nineveh. Thank You for another chance. In Jesus' Matchless Name, Amen.

Friendship Circle

"There are "friends" who pretend to be friends, but there is a friend who sticks closer than a brother." (Proverbs 18:24)

Sometimes the ones we think will stick with us do not. Every friendship is not deep and they will not all last forever. Some friendships, simply put, are shallow. But God is a friend who will never bail out on you. He promises to stay with you through the thick and the thin. I have found His promise to be true! Invite Him into your friendship circle, you will find Him faithful too!

Let's agree: Father, sometimes relationships are discouraging. It seems almost impossible to find a friend who is true. Help me to be discerning in my future friend selections. Send true friends my way; people who will encourage me when I'm down. I want friends with whom I can laugh and cry; people who will hurt when I hurt and celebrate my achievements with sincere joy. But at the end of the day Lord, *no one* will ever take Your place as my #1 Friend! You are my Best Friend. Thank You for my true friends, Father. Please bless them in a special way today. In Jesus' Name, Amen!

Equally Yoked

"Do not be yoked together with unbelievers. For what do righteousness and wickedness have in common? Or what fellowship can light have with darkness?" (2 Corinthians 6:14)

When it comes to relationships, God commands His children to choose from among believers, someone whose faith is consistent with His Word. In short, they should believe as you believe. He says that choosing an unbeliever is like inviting darkness into your life. As you know, light and darkness cannot coexist; therefore, introducing darkness into your space reduces your light, and the less light you have, the easier it is to be tripped up by the deceiver. May I suggest this simple nugget of relational wisdom…

In relationships seek to be:
Slow, safe, & satisfied
Rather than:
Fast, furious, & foolish

Let's agree: Father, first of all, thank You for the gift of marriage. As I filter my way through potential spouses, please help me to choose what is attractive to me, but also what is attractive to You. Send the right one my way Lord, and let me be at the right place at the right time doing what is right when we meet. Take away the spirit of anxiousness which can lead to developing relationships inconsistent with my faith. Help me to proceed through the dating process slowly, safely, and with great satisfaction that I am doing it right. In Jesus' Holy Name, Amen.

Be Vigilant!

"God blesses those who hunger and thirst for justice, for they will be satisfied." (Matthew 5:6)

Be vigilant in your commitment to justice for all. Don't allow God's plan for racial diversity, unity, and equality to become polluted by satan's plan for racial hate, separation, and injustice. Sunday morning must not continue to be the most segregated hour of the week; we must unite across racial and denominational lines. The enemy is cunning, he will use any means to divide and conquer the Church. Keep your spiritual and physical eyes open and fight for racial unity and equality every chance you get! May God's grace and protection keep you!

Let's agree: Father, although a month has been set aside on the calendar to focus on racial equality, help me to be mindful that the assignment I am on is not limited by man's understanding of time. You transcend time, and Your commands are unhindered by time zones and calendars. Therefore, my fight for racial justice must also effortlessly leap the fence of time and defeat hatred wherever it is found. Thank you Father for strength to endure and faith to overcome, for my hunger and thirst for righteousness will be satisfied. In Jesus' Name, Amen!

A Lesson In Gardening

"Don't worry about anything; instead, pray about everything. Tell God what you need, and thank him for all he has done. Then you will experience God's peace, which exceeds anything we can understand. His peace will guard your hearts and minds as you live in Christ Jesus." (Philippians 4:6, 7)

Gardening is one of my favorite pastimes. I acquired my love for beautiful flowers from two different generations, my mother and my grandmother. One lesson I learned over the years is that to keep weeds from taking over my garden I must install borders/boundaries that prevent them from spreading. This lesson also has application in life. Boundaries should be placed around the situations that burden us; limiting their ability to spread anxiety into other areas of our lives. This allows areas of life that are going well to continue to blossom, while we work on removing the weeds elsewhere. Weeds are situations that tempt us to worry; and they grow indiscriminately. You cannot keep them from popping up, not even with weed blocker and weed killing sprays. But you can reduce their number and frequency by placing strong barriers around your garden. So do not be discouraged when problems pop up in your life, put a boundary around them and work on de-weeding the area with time on your knees.

Let's pray: Father, thank You for the beauty of my life. Help me to realize that weeds can only diminish the beauty of the flowers of my life if I let them. Teach me to limit the distraction of the weeds and focus more on the flowers. You said I would have trials and tribulations, but You also promised to help me to overcome in every situation. This means I have victory over *every* weed in my life. Lord, both rain and warm sunshine are needed in every garden for the flowers to grow. Give me strength to pray, rain or shine. Remind me every day that life is too short to allow troubles to blind me to its beauty! In Jesus' Name, Amen!

Jumping To Conclusions

"Any story sounds true until someone tells the other side and sets the record straight." (Proverbs 18:17)

Have you ever formed conclusions about a situation before you had all of the details? I have, and the story is never as I thought it was once I hear the other side. We must remember that people will generally share details of any situation in a manner that makes them look best. It is naïve to expect them to do otherwise. Think about it, we likely do the same thing too. So, next time don't be naïve, get all the facts before you form your conclusions; it will show wisdom and maturity.

Let's agree: Father, give me the wisdom and patience to hear the whole story before making a judgment. I want to give people the benefit of a doubt until the evidence proves they are to be doubted. Thank You Lord for sharing Your wisdom with me. Help me to live by it every day! In Jesus' Righteous Name, Amen!

A Fresh Start

"And when sins have been forgiven, there is no need to offer any more sacrifices." (Hebrews 10:18)

Sometimes the biggest obstacle to moving past our mistakes is us. We feel so badly about what we have done that we choose to punish ourselves more harshly than God. By this I mean that even though you have asked God to forgive you, you continue to treat yourself as though you are unforgiven. This is a trick of the devil to keep you in the unproductive place of self-condemnation. He lies to you by telling you what you did was *so* bad that not even God is willing to forgive you. Believing this lie tosses us into a cycle of self-loathing one moment and crying for God's mercy the next. What God wants us to understand is that forgiveness is free! He knew that we would need more of it than we could afford, so He has made this priceless gift free of charge. Wouldn't it be nice if the world worked on that philosophy? There would be no wars, no poverty, and no greed. Well, we can keep praying about the world. But as far as God's forgiveness goes, it is still free, so accept it, thank Him for it and move on!

Let's agree: Father, thank You for forgiving me. I know I have made some pretty bad choices; selfish choices that have brought some painful consequences. I have been stubborn, proud, and headstrong. I do not know why. All I can say is thank You for washing away the stains. Thank You for giving me another chance to make the right decisions. Father, show me how to forgive myself. Help me to let go of the mistakes of the past and focus on the grand future You have planned for me. No more beating myself up, satan's done enough of that. Starting today I give myself the fresh start that Jesus died to give me. I forgive myself of EVERYTHING I have done wrong! Take my hand Father; let's walk together into that amazing future You have placed before me!!! In Jesus' Wondrous Name, Amen!

Challenge

"All praise to God, the Father of our Lord Jesus Christ. God is our merciful Father and the source of all comfort. He comforts us in all our troubles so that we can comfort others. When they are troubled, we will be able to give them the same comfort God has given us." (2 Corinthians 1:3,4)

In closing, here is a challenge. It would be easy to now put this devotional on the shelf and move on, but instead of doing what is easy join me as a wingman in God's "ARMY OF ENCOURAGERS". Become an intentional encourager inspiring people everywhere not to settle for just what is offered, but strive for what is best! If you know someone who is loaded down by life, give them the gift of encouragement; share a copy of Radically Living the Word. You will not regret it, and you just might receive the blessing you seek in the midst of being the blessing someone else needs. Take the challenge today!

Let's agree: Father, You are always so faithful to embrace me every day with Your encouraging Word. When I have been battered, broken, discouraged, disappointed, and at times, even doubtful, You have strengthened me with Your Word. Train my mind and my mouth to do the same for others. In Your Powerful Name, Amen!

Name:____

Sign me up!

*"Raise a signal flag on a bare hilltop.
Call up an army against Babylon.
Wave your hand to encourage them
as they march into the palaces of the high and mighty.*

Isaiah 13:2

A Gift of Encouragement

To:____

From:____

"I want them to be encouraged and knit together by strong ties of love. I want them to have complete confidence that they understand God's mysterious plan, which is Christ himself. [3] In him lie hidden all the treasures of wisdom and knowledge". (Colossians 2:2-3)

About the Author

Alice Richardson is a dynamic speaker, author, and biblical counselor. She earned her undergraduate degree from Oklahoma Christian University and holds a graduate degree in Biblical Counseling from Trinity Seminary. She has served in ministry for more than twenty years developing and leading ministries which meet both the practical and spiritual needs of believers and unbelievers alike.

Alice lives life in color. She has enjoyed playing collegiate athletics and served as a Division 1 Women's Basketball Official, a volunteer Basketball Coach, Chaplain, and Mentor. She retired from the United States Air Force Reserves as a Lieutenant Colonel after more than twenty-five years of honorable service to our country.

A sought after conference speaker, Alice uses her broad life experiences to refresh, encourage, and inspire. To her, life is a great adventure with countless opportunities to learn and grow. This means whether an experience brings tears or a smile, it has value to make our lives richer depending upon how we process it. Her prayer is for all people to accept the grace that God extends to each of us through His Son, and to live life walking in the love and power of His transformative Word.

To order additional copies or schedule engagements contact:
Website: www.alicerichardson.org
Email: alicetrichardson@gmail.com